The _____Encounter

Touched by God Chosen for Greatness

Joslyn E. Sanders

T.N.T. Publishing

Oakdale, Louisiana

Dedication

To God be the glory.

My Daddy is just...His wonders are innumerable. Faithful.
He just never ceases to amaze me on this pilgrimage. It's ALL
good! (Romans 8:28) I love you more today.

Evelyn Cleveland~ Mother, BFF, Rock, biggest supporter and a
steward of what God gave her...a girl. For no matter where I am
in life, on the top or bottom, you told me the TRUTH, never
judged me, and pushed me to be the woman I am today. I could
never give back all you have given me, so I ask God to do it for
me. I love you Mommie!

Grover Cleveland ~Daddy I find myself becoming you more
and more every day. LOL! You have always been my catalyst.
Pushing me to see all of my potential. I could not see it then but
I truly see it now. I thank God for it and you. I love you.

Dale Sanders Jr. ~ You are truly ONE of a kind. God could not
have created a more eccentric person to walk with me. You
push, encourage, and cover me. Thank you for loving my
imperfections perfectly. I love you babe!

To You. Yes you. You thought it well to purchase this project.
May it bring you wisdom, strength, courage and dismantle
every strongman holding you back from the next level.

Introduction

I believe we are living in the absolute most significant season the Body of Christ has ever known. It is a time in which God is revealing Himself to those who have remained faithful and obedient and He is pouring out an unusual anointing to penetrate the atmosphere of darkness on those who are willing to be equipped and used mightily for His glory. It is also however a time of great opposition. It is no secret that we are living in perilous and troubled times. We live in a time as believers where the world is making a mockery of everything we know to be truth. The enemy has infiltrated our government, our schools, our churches, our families, and the sanctity of marriage. The heart of man is filled with iniquity, fear, dread, frustration and despair.

Believers all across the country from every denomination, race, and gender are disillusioned, disappointed, and desperately trying to understand why they are no longer fulfilled by the mundane Sunday after Sunday church routine. They are experiencing a new and exciting hunger for God's presence and His Word, yet they are spiritually drained. They are searching for an explanation for the spiritual void and emptiness they are experiencing. Sadly, for the most part, the place they have turned to for the solution (the church) is not providing the answers.

The fact that we have arrived at this place in history is not by happenstance. This dark and desperate hour in our world is the believer's hour of destiny. We were born for such a time as this. The time has come to set into motion a mighty, sweeping, spiritual revolution that will change the game of the enemy and reveal to humanity that one touch, just one ENCOUNTER with Jesus is all we need to shake the foundations of this nation for the Kingdom.

From Adam and Eve in Genesis, to the Apostle John's trip to the throne room in Revelation, the bible is filled with accounts of one divine encounter after another. Moreover, just as the great men and women of the bible experienced these life-changing encounters with God, He wants you and me to experience the same. Not a Sunday morning shout and emotional charge experience, but a personal, remarkable, undeniable encounter with God marked by His presence and power that will bring repentance, renewed minds, transformed character, agape love, a fresh anointing, and a new boldness to walk in your God-ordained purpose.

In this book, Lady Joslyn Sanders gives a compelling charge to the reader to PUSH their way into purpose in contrast to perhaps the greatest and most talked about encounter with God ever recorded. It is the remarkable story of a little virgin girl from Nazareth who too was touched by God and chosen for greatness. Through Lady

Joslyn's story, you will find the fortitude and the stamina

to effectively walk in destiny and live out the call of God

on your life with courage, confidence, and power.

I make known the end from the beginning, from ancient times, what is still to come. I say, My purpose will stand, and I will do all that I please. Isaiah 46:10 (NIV)

Pastor Courtney Artiste

The Story of Mary
The Peculiar Pregnancy

I have loved the Lord as long as I can recall, it being the compass of my life considering my youth. He has reigned on the throne of my heart chambers, as the pilgrimage has been more than its share of rewarding.

So, here I am a virgin -Untouched & set apart
Been that way for quite some time and now this...

This encounter...

You see this I have never experienced. Don't get me wrong now...I love to bask in His arms but this is different. I have been chosen to perform a Holy thing. Not at all about to decline, but it's not just me anymore...

I am engaged to the man God has placed me with.

Lord knows I cannot mess this up. As I experienced this visitation, my heart took so many leaps and bounds. I just knew I had translated! My heart cried humility as I considered my frail humanity. Me? Conceive this Holy thing in my wound? Considering the lowliness of my circumstances, I pondered. I couldn't say no. If He came to me, I must have been the chosen one. What will they say of my marriage? Would they care? It doesn't matter because I choose to please Him. So, I gave my word for His...and

He Overshadowed me....

Cramps of Conception

Has God ever just done something in your life so out of the norm that it threw you for a loop? I am speaking of when you were so taken aback that you were puzzled. Well, that is what happened to the mother of Jesus………

Mary, the mother of Jesus, lived in the ghettos of Nazareth. Nazareth was not known for much. Same thing, day in and day out. No one famous or exceptional ever came from Nazareth, until now. Mary was reared in the ways of the Jehovah. She and her husband to be, Joseph, had customs of their time to be in separate households until they were married. In Nazareth, Joseph was known to be a just man and as we would say today, the cream of the crop. Perfect setup right? Equally yoked man and woman of God...keep reading because here comes the dilemma. This is where the plot thickens.

Mary is pregnant and Joseph knows he is not the father. He has never known Mary sexually and as far as he knows neither had any other man. Can you imagine how Joseph must have felt? The woman he loves and is about to marry is claiming Immaculate Conception. Is she a liar or just crazy? Maybe both! What is he to do? Joseph does not want to put her to shame. I should just put her away privately he thought. How is it that in the moment you find yourself in a situation, the very ones that you thought would be there fall back? This situation was serious. Mary was facing death and if Nazareth found out, she would be stoned by sunset. Joseph doubted his decision and Mary is cramping.

The cramps of conception are uncomfortable and painful. You have no control over them. They come unexpectedly and all you can do is brace yourself. Do you know what the worst part about it is? You are the only one that can feel the cramps. Joseph did not feel Mary's pain; he was merely a divine connection to destiny. Let me quickly interject; when choosing a mate, please be sure he or she is divinely connected to your destiny. You may have to take some unnecessary detours if they are not. Joseph obeyed the voice of the angel concerning Mary. If you are unequally yoked, they may not believe as you believe, see as you see, or hear what you hear. When Joseph accepted, he then covered his fiancé. God will provide a covering and you will not be made ashamed.

Conception takes place when you believe the Word for your life. Implantation happens when the seed of the Word has taken root and pain is the sign of the growth happening on the inside. I hear what you are saying, pain is not supposed to be evident of promise. Sweetheart, destiny is uncomfortable. It draws you out of what you know and into the unknown. The blessed part about that is, it is only unknown to YOU. God has already predestined you. Your Promise was spoken long before you were born. The Promise is coming!

Pregnant With Power

I remember first sensing my calling. It was at a depressing time in my life. I had things and people on the throne of my heart and not God. I had loved the Lord since my youth. I had wisdom beyond my years but I never quite fit in and I always found myself more alone than with friends yet I always drew a crowd...sound familiar to anyone? My heart really was towards God. However, my actions were quite different then my heart. I was allowing my flesh to lead. I was contemplating suicide. I felt exposed, naked, vulnerable, and afraid but it was an encounter with God at a river dam that I experienced a peace that snatched the spirit of suicide and dismantled it.

I received instant deliverance. In that moment, I realized that He was more real than I. I then understood that my life had reason. I conceived destiny that day and death loosed its grip on my life.

So now, back to Mary. The book of Luke gives us her story. Picture she is relaxing at home and suddenly an angel shows up in her living room and announces that she is favored among women. You did not hear me! I said God's messenger shows up in the ghettos of Nazareth with a divine announcement of favor. Can anything good come out of Nazareth? (LOL) My Lord, just when you are comfortable with where you are, divine declarations come. You were called to Purpose. Not only will you conceive it, but what you will carry will be GREAT. Know this; the Power you will carry framed the world you are operating in.

Nothing God does is small. You cannot be caught up in the mundane. You have Heaven at your disposal. The Kingdom is in you. YES YOU! I come against small mindsets and naysayers that will tell you "It does not take all of that." By the authority of the name of Jesus, you will never ever be the same after God speaks life into you. His Word is spirit and life. One Word from Heaven can redirect your destiny. If you can believe it, you can conceive it. It transformed my life and He is no respecter of persons.

So Mary's initial response was fear. Do not allow fear to abort your destiny. There is too much at stake. God wants you to conceive a Holy thing and you have to believe past what you see. You cannot walk into your destiny wondering "What if?" and "What will they think?" Your perspective of things makes all the difference. People's opinion should not sway you. You had better obey God baby. Fear is faith in reverse. It is you telling God that He cannot bring His will for your life to pass. Now listen at how ridiculous that sounds.

Mary discerned the angel's reason for being there. Gabriel was there to pronounce the pregnancy of the Savior. God will place a messenger in your life to give you direction through declaration. When God has purpose for your life, the Word adds to you! The angel calmed all of her fears. Fear not he spoke. Perfect love casts out all fear.

The Word of God is His love letter to us. A letter that says He can work a work in who will let Him. Declarations lay the road to destiny.

The Holy Spirit is waiting on you right now. You may not believe that, but He is. His desire is that you be Overshadowed. That the manifested power of God enter your womb. You are positioned for power. Mary recognized it was not of herself. "Be IT unto me..." was her response to the declaration. What is IT? It is The Word God speaks into you to birth your destiny. Be it unto me according to thy Word...POWER ACTIVATED! This power was confirmed months later when she visited her cousin Elisabeth. When Mary greeted Elisabeth, who was also pregnant, Elisabeth's baby LEAPED in her wound.

She spoke a Word over Mary and confirmation of the POWER within her was declared.

Confirmation comes to keep you on track to divine destiny. A renowned Prophet by the name of Kelvin Hall was in town and I felt an overwhelming tugging in my spirit to go to the service even though it had already begun. I do not like to attend worship late. It vexes me not to be on time but I arrived as the man of God was introducing the text and just as I had sensed, I was divinely routed there. His message entitled, Hide My Child, was about this very thing. It spoke of protecting the Promise. The very anointing that is on your life is precious. The enemy desires to abort the Power. You were born for this moment and for such a time as this. You must guard the Power. Throughout Mary's pregnancy, the Power consistently grew inside of her. And every now and then, there was movement to confirm the presence of it! Can you imagine how she may have felt? You too are pregnant with Power. Guard your Promise because you are almost there!

Pushing the PROMISE

I have not yet had the privilege of carrying a child of my own, so I personally have not had the natural experience of birthing. However, I coached a young lady who gave birth to her daughter in the backseat of my car! That along with the spiritual births I have encountered, I would say I have some experience under my belt (LOL). I imagine the joys of pregnancy are very rewarding. Your body transitions to bring forth, your appetite changes to accommodate the extra, and your mindset changes as you anticipate the arrival of the baby. It is the same way with spiritual births. You do not continue in the same mindset you had before you got the news. You are packing something divine dear heart. You become protective in nature. You watch what you do and how you do it. You redirect your life because you are expecting. You have a glow about you. My goodness I get excited just thinking about it.

By now, Mary is almost due. There is a tax to be paid so she and her husband head into Judea to Jerusalem. Mary goes into labor. They try to find a room at the inn yet all the rooms are booked. No clean bed to have this Child? Inn after inn and no room. Let me speak into your life in this season. The reason there is no room at your inn is because a room cannot contain what you are getting ready to deliver! There was no room for Mary because her Promise was for the World. Glory to God! Your Promise is for nations and foreign soils you have yet to tread upon and for people you have yet to meet. Of course, there will not be a room! (Yes, Lord I thank You!)

So an innkeeper feels sorry and says there is a stable out back. A stable? I thought, The Savior of the world born in a stable, in a manger where animals feed-ewwwww! That was until I got the revelation of the stable. Jesus was The Lamb that was to be slain to reverse the curse. Animal sacrifices were coming to an end. Why do you think the shepherds had to visit? He was The Lamb! And where are lambs born? A stable! Mary drops down, undoubtedly yelling at Joseph, the pain is intense but she feels something, she is crowning! The head is visible now. Joseph tells Mary to PUSH! Any nurse can tell you that this part of delivery is most the painful because something is coming out of you. This is also a most dangerous time because your life and the life you are delivering is at stake. Do not abort the PROMISE. Do not let the promise die because of the PAIN. Don't you dare stop PUSHING! I know things seem crazy, they are talking about you, and your bills are overtaking you but PUSH! You received a divine Word to take it to a new level but you stopped pushing because of the external noise but baby I am going to need you to push! That Promise cannot die now. You have come too far and lost too much. Lives are at stake here. Lives will be lost if you do not PUSH! Think about those connected to you, just like an unborn child, if you die then they will too. Can you hear your Joseph? PUSH

PUSH!

And just when you thought you could not make it another day, or push another push there it is. THE PROMISE will arrive and it will be all you expected and more. But wait, where is the pain? You will find that it is gone! Why? The PROMISE is here! Congratulations on your new arrival! I am excited for you.

Destiny Workbook

Encountering God

When we think of an experience with God, we usually think of dramatic angelic visitations with lightning bolts and fog or miracles like the parting of the Red Sea or people being raised from the dead. However, God reveals Himself to us in many ways and it is rarely the way we predict He will. God created you. He knows everything about you, including your level and method of comprehension. God does not want you confused or perplexed. He wants to communicate with you in a way that you can understand and in a way that will bring lasting change and transformation. Never feel less spiritual or insignificant because God chooses to communicate with you in a way that is different from someone else. He reveals Himself to different people at different times in different situations in many different ways.

Think about it….There are seven billion people on this planet all created by God and not one of them exactly alike. Even identical twins are different biologically and has at least one distinguishing characteristic. That can only mean that God is One Creative Guy to be able to design seven billion people and counting uniquely, so take Him out of the box concerning His communication with you. He is God, the creator and ruler of all so He is not limited to your thinking or your expectations. It is highly unlikely that Mary expected to be a pregnant virgin let alone pregnant with the Savior of the World. Aren't you glad God was not moved by her expectations? I sure am.

Hindrances to Divine Encounters

- Not filled with the Holy Spirit
- Not Hearing The Voice of God
- Lack of faith
- Preconceived Expectations
- Over-spiritualizing
- Disobedience
- Sin
- Unforgiveness/Bitterness

Some ways to encounter God

- Salvation
- Healing/Deliverance
- Audible voice
- Invasive thoughts (thoughts you just cannot "shake")
- Proxy/Prophet
- His Word
- Visions
- Angelic visitation
- Situations/Circumstances
- Miracles
- Dreams

As we look through the scriptures we can see, repeatedly how those, regardless of their religious or ethnic backgrounds, unrighteous choices, or past mistakes, had encounters with God, and were radically changed. Let's study a few. Study the scriptures about these men and women of God and jot down significant facts such as their background, social status, specifics of their initial encounter, their response/reaction, what they were called to do, and the outcome.

1. Abram later Abraham- Genesis 11:27-25:8

_____

_____

_____

_____

_____

_____

_____

_____

_____

2. Gideon- Judges 6:1-8-8:32

_____

_____

_____

_____

_____

_____

_____

_____

_____

3. Rahab- Joshua 2:2-21 ,6:17,23,25

_____

_____

_____

_____

_____

_____

_____

_____

_____

4. Jonah- The book of Jonah

_____

_____

_____

_____

_____

_____

_____

_____

5. Nehemiah- The book of Nehemiah

_____

_____

_____

_____

_____

_____

_____

_____

6. Esther- The book of Esther

_____

_____

_____

_____

_____

_____

_____

_____

_____

7. Woman at the Well- John 4:7-42

_____

_____

_____

_____

_____

_____

_____

_____

8. Saul/Paul- Acts 7:58-8-3, 9:1-30

9. Widow of Zarephath- 1 Kings 17:9-24

10. Ananias & Sapphira- Acts 5:1-10

_____

_____

_____

_____

_____

Although each of these encounters were vastly different in nature, they all have two common denominators, transformed character, and a fresh anointing, and unfortunately some have a not pleasant characteristic..............

Application

- Which of the people studied above do you most identify yourself with? Why?
- Recall in detail a divine experience or encounter with the Lord?
- Recall your response/reaction?
- What was the outcome?

****Just in case you had a divine encounter with God and He gave you a directive or instructions that you did not follow. Do not beat yourself up about it! Repent and get moving today!

Thief of Destiny

Fear is an EMOTION (take note of this fact) brought on by a PERCEIVED threat, meaning you sense that which you are fearful of will harm you. Most often, you will find that it is just that….perceived and you were never in any real danger at all. Yet, many modern day Moses', Esther's, Nehemiah's, Elijah's, Joshua's Caleb's and Paul's have averted their opportunity to leave their mark on the world because of this little four-letter word. It is the supreme thief of purpose and destiny and perhaps the enemy's most lucrative device.

According to an internet source, there are more than 530 documented phobias. That is a lot of fear running loose. Among those are two I call mental fears, the fear of rejection and failure. Mental fears cannot cause physical harm but if not checked, will wreck shop on you emotionally and mentally and stunt your growth. These two wiles of the enemy are stripping believers all over the world of their destiny and purpose at an alarming rate. "They will say I've changed". I'll lose all of my friends". "What if it doesn't work? "No one has ever done it before". These thoughts are the hearse that has driven many witty inventions, brilliant ideas, and solutions to problems to the purpose graveyard.

It is critical to understand that fear comes from the enemy. 2 Timothy 1:7 says, *"For God hath not given us the spirit of fear; but of power, and of love, and of a sound mind".* Fear is ultimately bondage and leaves you stagnant and paralyzed. However, as we can see from the great men and women studied earlier, fear is a natural reaction when your call is great. God understood this. The phrase "fear not" is mentioned in the bible over 60 times. Certain levels of fear are "normal". Everyone experiences fear of rejection and or failure to some degree at some point in his or her lives. No one likes failure or the feeling of being rejected especially by people they love, but you must value your dreams and the vision God has given you over the opinion of anyone. You must trust that God who begun this work in you is able to bring it to fruition. Some of you reading this have not been aware of the fear holding you back. Perhaps it has disguised itself as cautiousness or prudence. Whatever mask it wears, you must take an honest assessment of your life and if its fear that is keeping you from being obedient to the voice of God, it must be eradicated in order for you to walk in your destiny and be the person God has called you to be.

Identifying Fear of Failure & Rejection

- Do you shy away from change?
- Do you shy away from meeting new people?
- Do you avoid risks?
- Do you make excuses for your failures?
- Do you worry what people will say about your failures?
- Are you a people pleaser?
- Are you passive aggressive?
- Do you avoid dating/marriage?

Stomp the Life out of Fear and Move into Destiny

One of the first scriptures I learned concerning my authority as a believer was 2 Corinthians 10:5. The Message translation says, "*We use our powerful God-tools for smashing warped philosophies, tearing down barriers erected against the truth of God, fitting every loose thought and EMOTION (remember that word?) *and impulse into the structure of life shaped by Christ*". We have to control our emotions. God will not do that for us. Philippians 4:8 says, *"Finally brethren, whatsoever things are true, whatsoever things are honest, whatsoever things are just, whatsoever things are pure, whatsoever things are lovely, whatsoever things are of good report; if there* *be any virtue, if there be any praise, think on these things".* According to 2 Corinthians 10:5, we (with the help of the Holy Spirit) have to bring our loose thoughts and emotions into captivity and make them obedient to Philippians 4:8. There is one sure-fire way to control emotions and that is to control your thoughts because fear always begins with a thought. Control my thoughts? How can I possibly do that? I am so glad you asked!

Information starts with environmental stimuli that enter our sensory memory through our sight, hearing, or touch. That information then leaves the sensory memory and enters the short-term memory (the mind). Information that you do not attend to is lost. Simply put, it is forgotten. Only by rehearsal can information pass from the short-term memory to the long-term memory (the heart). So it is with fear. This is the principle of repetition. The consistent rehearsal of that fearful thought enables it to leave your mind and enter your heart causing fear to grip you. Thankfully principles work both ways because just as easily as you can rehearse the negative thoughts of fear (or any thought not in align with God's Word), you can sabotage them by saturating your mind with the Word of God and simple consistent faith confessions. So, when the thoughts of doubt and pessimism arise, simply evict it with the Word of God. For example, when the thought "I can't start my own ministry or business because I'm not smart enough or God can't use someone like me" arises, immediately shoot it down with

Philippians 4:13, *"I can do all things through Christ who strengthens me"*.

The tongue is a powerful weapon that we must use against the enemy. Matthew 11:23 says, *"For verily I say unto you, That whosoever shall SAY unto this mountain, Be thou removed, and be thou cast into the sea; and shall not doubt in his heart, but shall believe that those things which he saith shall come to pass; he SHALL HAVE whatsoever he SAITH"*. A simple faith confession (intentionally speaking life-filled words in agreement with God's Word) said on a consistent basis can stomp the life out of fear and get you moving towards your destiny.

Another way to put fear on the run is by focusing on the reward. After giving Abram the directive to leave his home and his kin to go to a strange land in Genesis 12:1, God immediately speaks to Him about the blessings associated with his obedience in Genesis 12:2-3. Now why do you think He did that? Some super saints would like you to think that focusing on the blessing is ungodly or selfish. If this were so, why would God go into such detail about the blessing? You ask such great questions!

When God gives an instruction, He often reveals the reward or the blessing before He reveals the process it will take to get it done. Malachi 3:10 says, *"Bring ye all the tithes into the storehouse, that there may be meat in mine house, and prove me now herewith, saith the Lord of hosts, if I will not open you the windows of heaven, and pour you out a blessing, that there shall not be room enough to receive it".* Here we see a COMMAND to tithe yet there is blessing attached. He does not tell us that the enemy will fight us in the area of our giving, or that there will be times when in the natural it would make much more sense not to, but He goes straight into the blessing. Even Jesus in the Garden of Gethsemane requested an easier route to destiny but Hebrews 12:2 says who for the joy set before Him endured the cross and despised the shame. You see the joy set before him was you and I standing in our rightful place totally redeemed and reconciled to God. The reward or the blessing is what motivates you to action and action annihilates fear. It is the anchor that keeps you grounded when the enemy sends thoughts of give-up to your mind. We go to work when our bodies are physically and mentally fatigued for the reward of payday and to be able to buy the things we need and want. Athletes practice despite their achy bodies and sore muscles for the reward of finishing as champions. We receive salvation and walk out that salvation daily to win others for the Kingdom and to spend eternity with Jesus. We are reward-oriented beings and God is perfectly okay with that. After all, it is the way He designed us and that is why it is not selfish or ungodly to do what God called you to do with the reward or blessing as the motivation to keep PUSHING.

In the final pages of this book, you will find The Daily Destiny Confession and the 21-Day Destiny Journal. Research has shown that anything done consistently for

21 days becomes a habit. Make a commitment to spend a minimum of 21 days confessing the Destiny Confession and journaling your encounters with the Lord and watch how your relationship with Him intensifies. Journaling works best if done at the beginning of your day and then again at the end of the day, but how you do it is not important. That is entirely up to you and God. If there are days in which you feel as if the Lord has not spoken to you that is quite okay. We have all been there. Instead, record a dream you may have had (always record dreams they are very significant in this season), a scripture to meditate on, your thoughts, emotions (good and bad), and how you dealt with them. Were there situations that you could have handled differently? Can you identify sure areas that

could be standing between you and your destiny such as fear, laziness, or procrastination? Ask the Lord to teach you how to make the necessary adjustments to your life and how you can make your life and the life of someone else better than the day before. Let the Holy Spirit be your guide.

In closing, know that you are powerful beyond anything you can imagine and God is able to do exceeding, abundantly above all that you can ask or think in and through you. You have been waiting on God but He is waiting on you. You are free to operate in the miracle working power of the Holy Spirit. The clarion call has been sounded and your destiny awaits. Will you go get it? I pray you will! *Be Encouraged, Be Empowered, & Walk in Victory.*

Destiny Confession

Father I trust Your Word that says You know the plans You have for me. Plans to give me hope and a future. I thank You that Your word is a lamp unto my feet and a light unto my path. I thank You that I am sensitive to Your will and I submit myself to Your authority. I acknowledge You in all my ways and You direct my path. Thank You for Your precious Holy Spirit who guides me and teaches me Your will for my life. I have the ability to bring every thought, action, and emotion that exalts itself above You into captivity and command it to obey. I can do all things through Christ who strengthens me so I am not afraid. I have power, love and a sound mind. I have the fortitude and stamina to PUSH my way into my destiny. I am an anointed, chosen vessel of the Lord. I obey the Father's voice and I am set apart to do His will so His plans for me are established. I have the Spirit of Wisdom and revelation in the knowledge of Him. The eyes of my understanding are enlightened and I know the hope of His calling. I live an intentional life. I am bold and strong, and I am more than a conqueror and I walk in DESTINY & PURPOSE every moment of every day of my life. I am committed to helping others do the same-In Jesus Name

21-Day Destiny Journal

Day 1

_____

_____

_____

_____

_____

_____

_____

Day 2

_____

_____

_____

_____

_____

_____

_____

_____

_____

Day 3

Day 4

Day 5

Day 6

Day 7

Day 8

Day 9

Day 10

_____

_____

_____

_____

_____

_____

_____

_____

Day 11

Day 12

Day 13

Day 14

Day 15

Day 16

Day 17

Day 18

Day 19

Day 20

Day 21

21 Day Reflection

_____

_____

_____

_____

_____

_____

_____

_____

_____

_____

_____

_____

_____

_____

_____

_____

_____

_____

Prophetic Word

By
Pastor Courtney Artiste

I believe that we are on the horizon of the greatest spiritual revival man has ever known. God is assembling and equipping a remnant of uncommon radical and totally sold out believers with no other agenda than to advance the Kingdom by exhibiting the Love of Jesus to lead that revival. I believe those believers are sensing that God is calling them to do something very significant. He is calling them to step into their destiny and take their rightful place in the Kingdom. He is showing you snippets of what is to come in your dreams and visions. Dreams are very very very important in this season so make record of them. He is connecting you with other members of the remnant and disconnecting you from those who are not. He is sanctifying, purging and pruning you in this season because this calling will require a greater level of faith, obedience, and submission.

Keep your eyes open the enemy senses the shift and he is not happy. He seeks to snuff you out, defame your character, and scandalize your name. Keep your hearts clean from unforgiveness, bitterness, grief, and sin. You were born for this. He has made you a fortified city, an iron pillar, and bronze walls against the whole land. Against the kings of Judah against its princes and its priests and against the people of the land. They will fight against you but they shall not prevail against you for He is with you to deliver you. Thus saith The Lord.

Joslyn Sanders, affectionately known as Joy is a wife, minister, practical nurse, and author. She resides in Oberlin, LA. She serves as an associate minister at St. John Baptist Church in Kinder, LA, where her husband Dale Sanders Jr. serves as Pastor. She is active in the church choir and partners with her husband in ministry. Her heart is empowering the people of God to see as God sees and reflect the glory of God in everyday life.

Joy has an unusual anointing that draws individuals to share their personal situations in ministry. Diverse and knowledgeable in the Word, she enjoys using colors, props and herself to get you "in" the message to gain victory and deliverance through the message of Jesus Christ. Her confident, nurturing, and transparent spirit is one you will never forget.

Lady Joslyn is available to speak at your next event; workshops, conferences, small and large women gatherings, place of business and seminars. Visit her website for booking info.

www.ladysanders.com

If you would like more information on becoming a published author in six months or less email T.N.T. Publishing at tntpublishingco@yahoo.com

Made in the USA
San Bernardino, CA
15 February 2014